Leadership Style, Toxic Leadership, Micromanagement, and Organizational Culture

Louis Bevoc

Published by
NutriNiche System LLC

Louis Bevoc books...simple explanations of complex subjects

Leadership Style

Introduction

Leaders are arguably the most critical aspect of any organization because they make decisions that dramatically impact workplaces. Their decisions implement policies and procedures, establish structure and hierarchy, dictate change, and shape culture. In short, leaders have a major bearing on the way organizations survive, operate, and progress.

Leaders of large organizations need to delegate tasks. They choose managers to carry out their plans, and those plans eventually find their way to the rank and file employees. Directives have the potential to get distorted during this process due to miscommunication, but over time the operations of the organization typically reflect the ideas of leadership.

Small organizational leaders typically have more influence than those in larger organizations. Think about a football team as an analogy. Small organizational leaders play the role of quarterback, coach, and owner. They hire the players, design the plays, and choose the game strategy. Their role is so important that one major decision can make or break their team...and that is a lot of weight for one person to carry on his or her shoulders.

Regardless of the size of an organization, all leaders have management styles that affect their behavior and decision making. These styles can be broken down into types, and that is the focus of the next section.

Types

Leadership style is a leader's approach to implementing ideas, establishing change, and managing people. In other words, it is his or her approach to running an organization.

Leaders use styles that work best for them, but they are not set in stone. Styles can change if necessary, depending on the situation. For example, a normally democratic leader might change her style to autocratic when reacting to a crisis.

This section breaks leadership style into specific types, and it follows a basic protocol for each analysis. First, the type is described for simplified understanding. Next advantages and disadvantages are listed to show the associated pros and cons. Last, but certainly not least, an organizational example is used to indicate real-world application.

Please consider the following types of style:

Authoritarian

These leaders want their organizations to be as efficient as possible, and they believe order and structure are the best way to achieve efficiency. Direct supervision is important and subordinates are kept on a tight leash. Policies and procedures are strictly followed, relationships are professional, and communication flows from top to bottom.

Authoritarian leaders focus on control. They maintain close supervision so they do not lose control, and they see other types of leadership style (such as democratic) as inefficient because control is limited.

Government agencies often use authoritative leadership styles because they want to maintain tight control. An example is a US border patrol supervisor. He makes sure his subordinates follow rules precisely, and he does not let allow them to make decisions without his approval.

Advantages

One advantage of an authoritarian leadership style involves orderliness. There is little opportunity for disorder or chaos because strict controls are in place. Things tend to remain in proper order from start to finish, and this eliminates confusion.

Another advantage of this style involves communication. Since most orders are direct, there is limited room for distorted messages, and miscommunication is less frequent than that experienced with other leadership styles.

Disadvantages

Probably the biggest disadvantage to the authoritarian leadership style is it creates a climate of fear. Employees are afraid to argue or question decisions made by authoritarian leaders because they might be jeopardizing their jobs.

Another disadvantage is the fact that creativity and diversity are stifled. Employees are not entitled to opinions, and there is no room for debate or disagreement. There is only one right answer...and it comes from the authoritarian leader.

Organizational example

Bertram owns a tool and die shop, and he uses an authoritarian style to lead his employees. When he makes business decisions, he does not consult anyone else. He makes choices based on his perception of the situation, and he is not open to people who challenge his decisions.

One good thing about Bertram's company is the fact that employees know what is expected of them. Bertram makes decisions that are cut-and-dry, and he never leaves people wondering about the direction they need to take. His direct orders are very clear and miscommunication is limited.

However, there are also some problems associated with Bertram's leadership style. He has made some decisions that his managers knew were wrong, but they did not challenge him due to the fear of retribution. They know Bertram does not take kindly to disagreement or criticism, and he does not allow debate about his choices. This is demoralizing to Bertram's managers because they feel like they have no freedom and their opinions do not matter. It has also resulted in some costly mistakes that could have been prevented with some discussion.

There are positive and negative effects associated with Bertram's leadership style. His tight control keeps the business organized, and this is important for running efficiency. However, it also suppresses the individuality of his managers and prevents healthy debate.

Democratic

Democratic leaders share decision-making responsibilities with other employees. They believe in debate, and they encourage discussion. This leadership style allows employees to feel good about themselves and the fact that they are involved in decision-making processes. Democratic leaders view authoritarian leadership as far too rigid with no room for new ideas or creativity.

One important and often overlooked aspect of this style is the fact that democratic leaders maintain control over the company and the employees within it. They decide who participates in the decision-making, and typically this does not include everyone. Additionally, these leaders will make decisions without other people's input if necessary. If discussions get off track or suggestions do not make sense, then democratic leaders will take charge.

Democratic leadership works well in organizations where workers are skilled and need little direction. An example is a company that does graphic design. All of the designers are capable of doing their jobs with limited supervision, and they also need to be creative.

Advantages

Democratic leadership motivates people and improves productivity because people get to voice their thoughts and opinions. Solutions to problems are more creative and diverse due to the wide variety of people involved. This style of leadership also encourages constant improvement because employees feed off each other's ideas during discussion.

Disadvantages

The downside of the democratic leadership style is that it is not applicable to every organization. It works well with skilled employees, but not so well with those who lack skills. For example, a manufacturing facility staffed with temporary employees would not be productive under democratic leadership. Employees simply do not know enough about their jobs to work without supervision, and their knowledge is too limited to be involved in decision-making processes.

Organizational example

Janice is the CEO of a toy manufacturer. She uses a democratic leadership style for the marketing department, and this has been very successful for the company. The freedom given to the marketing employees allows them to be creative, and they always have valuable input for new product ideas.

Democratic leadership works well for the marketing department of the toy manufacturer, but it does not have the same effect in other areas of the company. Janice cannot apply this style to production departments because these employees need direction in order to properly perform work-related tasks. Supervisors are needed to control the day-to-day activities and maintain efficiency. Additionally, production employees' knowledge is often limited to their specific job...so it is difficult to involve them in decision-making that impacts the entire company.

Democratic leadership is valuable at the toy company, but not in every department. Marketing personnel work very well under this style because they understand their job requirements, and they possess the knowledge to make good decisions. However, supervisors are needed to maintain efficiency in production because employees are less skilled, and their knowledge is often limited to a specific job.

Laissez-faire

This leadership style lets employees make all decisions. The "hands-off" approach puts power into the hands of rank and file personnel with very little direction from management.

Leadership's role is to provide the tools and materials necessary for employees to perform their jobs. Once employees have the necessary resources, leaders' roles are reduced to that of mentors. Essentially they need to:

1. Make themselves available if their assistance is required
2. Provide feedback after completion of the job or task

This style of leadership might seem like it would produce a chaotic and confusing work environment. However, this is typically not the case because management is available when needed, and they provide feedback about employee performance. In short, laissez-faire workplaces are the epitome of self-governance.

Advantages

A laissez-faire leadership style promotes a climate of trust. Workers basically manage themselves, and this creates a two-way trust between management and employees. Management trusts employees to do their jobs correctly, and employees trust management to let them do whatever is needed to complete tasks. Additionally, employees become better at making the right decisions as they become more experienced, and this further lessens the need for management support.

Disadvantages

The biggest disadvantage of this style of management is it will not work in many organizations. For laissez-faire leadership to be effective, all employees need to be educated, skilled, and experienced. This is typically not the case in the average workplace. Many employees need supervision to complete job tasks because they are not capable of doing everything on their own.

Additionally, this style will not work if leaders do not provide appropriate feedback. While direct supervision is not necessary, management needs to review and comment on jobs after they are completed. Employees who do not receive input from management might not be working toward achieving organizational goals and objectives.

Organizational example

Lester is the president of a farmer's coop. Every member manages their own farm, and they all market their products through the coop. Lester' role is to answer member questions regarding the business of farming and to provide feedback on the products they sell to the coop's customer base.

Fran is a member of the coop who raises wheat. She understands the growing of her product very well, but sometimes she needs help buying supplies for her farm. Lester knows a lot of people in the farm supply business, and he is able to answer Fran's questions.

Lester also provides helpful information to Fran after she sells her products through the coop. He makes her aware of customer comments regarding the quality of her wheat so she can make adjustments if necessary.

In short, Lester allows Fran to run her farm without his interference. He makes himself available to answer questions when his assistance is needed, but he remains mostly in the background. After Fran sells her product, Lester provides her with feedback from customers so she can make the adjustments necessary to meet the coop objective of selling high-quality products.

Paternalistic

Paternalistic leaders are exactly what the word implies...they act as a parent to the employees. They are more like a father figure than a supervisor because they take charge of their workers' lives inside and outside of work. They show concern by supporting employee ideas, protecting their best interests, encouraging them to give their best effort, and providing rewards for their success. In return, they expect loyalty from their employees...just like parents expect from children.

Advantages

The biggest advantage of the paternalistic leadership style is it builds self-confidence. Employees work hard due to their loyalty to the organization, and this pays off in terms of goal accomplishment. A feeling of success develops as they move on to their next task, and they build the self-confidence necessary to accomplish other goals. Essentially, a positive cycle results where employees build confidence, attain goals, and help the organization achieve objectives.

A major problem with this style of leadership involves workplace favoritism. Management tends to favor the employees who are the most loyal to the organization. Favoritism is not uncommon with other management styles, but it is more severe with paternalistic leaders because loyalty is so important.

Organizational example

Margaret is the owner of an art studio that creates stone sculptures. She has owned the studio for 30 years, and she has sold sculptures all over the world. She employs five people, and they have all worked for her for at least ten years.

Margaret manages her employees using a paternalistic leadership style. She treats them all like family. She socializes with them outside of work, attends their family functions, and even vacations with them. Her employees think of her as their mother, rather than their boss. They completely trust her, and they are extremely loyal to her. Their trust also helps them become successful artists, and it helps the studio grow and prosper.

Margaret's leadership behavior works well to build trust and loyalty, but it is not without drawbacks. She highly values employee loyalty and often favors the workers who are the most loyal. This causes internal stress as employees compete to be her favorite. Since that favorite can easily change, there is often a "flavor of the month" feeling among her staff.

In short, Margaret treats her employees like family because she manages them using a paternalistic leadership style. This style has pros and cons because it develops trust and builds employee confidence, but it also encourages unhealthy competition for her approval.

Transactional

Transactional leaders use rewards and punishment to influence employee behavior. They use rewards when performance meets or exceeds expectations, and they use punishment when performance is below expectations. Rewards are typically monetary, material, or psychological...the idea is simply to recognize performance achievements. Punishment usually involves corrective action and a plan for improvement...the idea is to eliminate the problem and progress toward satisfactory performance.

Transactional leaders believe in rules and standardized practices. They like to develop systems and hold employees accountable for meeting established standards. Unlike other leadership styles, such as democratic, they prefer the status quo and typically do not like change. Efficiency, flow, and productivity rank above everything else...and the best way to maximize these variables is to establish goals and objectives.

Advantages

One advantage of this type of leadership style is simplicity. Rewards and punishments are easily understood by all employees without training or detailed explanation.

Another advantage involves speed. Rewards are an instantaneous motivator for employees. When used correctly, they can improve workplace morale at crucial times.

Disadvantages

Management must have a constant presence in order for this leadership style to be successful. Success or failure of employees is dependent upon management appraisal...and they cannot appraise if they are not present. Additionally, when management is not around, employees might resort to deviant behavior to avoid punishment for not achieving organizational goals.

Another negative of transactional leadership involves rewards. Rewards are powerful motivators that can improve morale in critical periods. However, the increase in morale is only temporary. The positive perception of the reward wears off in a relatively short period of time, and employees can return to thinking negatively about their jobs and the organization. In other words, the inspirational effects of rewards are short-term.

Organizational example

Beverly is the president of a safety supply company, and she uses a transactional approach to leadership in order to keep things as simple as possible for her employees. She rewards salespeople who achieve pre-determined performance levels with bonuses, and she documents improvement plans for those who do not achieve the established levels. Salespeople who receive the bonuses are motivated to keep performing at high levels, and those who do not receive them are put on a plan to help them reach designated goals.

Beverly's leadership style works well because it is clearly understood by all of the salespeople. They do not need detailed explanation or training to know what is expected of them, and they know what they need to do in order to receive a bonus. These bonuses, however, do have a drawback. They work well as short-term motivators, but that motivation wears off in a few days. At that point, the salespeople need to draw from other inspiration or they lose the desire to sell safety supplies.

In short, Beverly uses a reward system that is motivating and easy to understand. However, the motivation is short-lived...and then employees need another source of inspiration to perform at optimum levels. Her transactional leadership style has pros and cons for her business, but it is where she finds comfort as a leader.

Transformational

Transformational leaders are typically knowledgeable and charismatic. They work tirelessly to get personnel to think independently about what is best for the organization. This is accomplished by setting objectives that drive employees to work harder and increase performance. In short, the goal of this leadership style is to "transform" employee thinking so they want to work toward improving the organization and taking it to the next level.

Advantages

Transformational leaders are visionaries because they are able to assess challenging situations and formulate plans for improvement. Their charismatic personalities work well to persuade employees to help them put their plans into action and achieve success. These individuals work well under adverse conditions, and they are often the best choice for a leader when an organization is experiencing difficult times.

Disadvantages

Transformational leaders are not very detail-oriented because they tend to focus on the big picture. Their lack of attention to detail can negatively affect the long-term vision they have in mind...even to the point where it does not work.

Additionally, these leaders are not always honest about their organization. Their charismatic personalities and passion for their vision often cause them to ignore reality. If employees detect this dishonesty, they can lose faith and trust in the leader's objectives.

Organizational example

Frank owns a pawn shop in a large metropolitan area. He is a very charismatic individual and knows his business well. His personality and business savvy have helped him grow the business to a point of stability, and now he plans to take it to the next level by putting an addition on his building and doubling his inventory.

Frank works hard to get his employees on board with his expansion plan. He tells them how much better the business will be after it expands and how the increased revenue will make it easier to give them raises. His rhetoric is well received by the workers, and they develop a positive outlook about the proposed growth.

Frank's charismatic personality does a good job persuading his employees, and they start to work harder to make his vision a reality. However, Frank has not been totally honest about everything happening in the company. He has not told his workers that local police have been watching the business because he has been accused of buying stolen goods. If employees find out about this issue, they might lose trust in Frank and his plan.

In short, Frank's charismatic personality gets his employees to work harder as they try to implement his expansion plan. However, he is not telling them about an important negative aspect of the business because his transformational leadership style prevents him from being completely honest.

Several different types of leadership styles are discussed above. Each type is described, advantages and disadvantages are noted, and an organizational example is presented for real-world application.

Most organizational leaders in today's world adhere to one of the styles discussed, but the world is changing as workplaces become more global and technologically advanced. That being said, leaders also need to change the way they manage in order to keep pace. For this reason, the future of leadership style needs to be examined...and that will be done in the next section.

Future

The world is constantly evolving, and this creates new opportunities and challenges for organizations. In order to keep pace in the future, leaders of organizations will need to assess the circumstances and undergo change. This leads to some important questions. What type of leaders will be needed in the future? What role will they play? Will the various leadership styles be necessary or will they become passé?

The answers to the above questions will now be explored by examining each type of leadership style. Please consider the following:

Authoritarian

There will be a need for authoritarian leadership in the future...regardless of whether or not people like it. It provides vision, and vision is necessary for wandering organizations...even if it comes at the expense of employee freedom. However, the popularity of this leadership style is unlikely to increase simply because so many people do not like working in controlled environments with rigid structures.

Advantages

This style of leadership will be helpful for organizations that are performing poorly because employees are not working together toward a clear and common goal. It unifies people and provides direction by creating order through structure and discipline.

Disadvantages

The biggest problem with authoritarian leadership will be that employees do not want to be tightly restricted. Quite simply, people need freedom and creativity at work in order to find job satisfaction. That feeling exists today, and it will not change in the future.

Democratic

This leadership style will be popular in the future because employees like to participate and be actively involved in decision making. Management likes the democratic style because it promotes debate, brings about positive change, and encourages constant improvement.

Advantages

As organizations become more global, they will turn into melting pots for diversity. This is good because different people and cultures offer a wide variety of solutions to problems. Democratic leadership will be the best way to manage a diverse workforce because it meets the involvement needs of all employees.

Disadvantages

As technology increases, people will understand even less about their jobs. They will need to rely more on supervision, and their limited knowledge will not allow them to be involved in decision-making processes. When this happens, the democratic style of leadership will not be a viable choice.

Laissez-faire

This leadership style will likely gain future value because employees will be more educated and skilled. Organizations will become less willing to train on the job because skilled people from all over the world will be available for employment. Technology has made telecommuting a reality for millions of people, and this adds to the significance of the laissez-faire leader.

Advantages

Laissez-faire leadership will promote employee decision making without management intervention. When this happens, employees will become better at making good decisions that benefit the organization, and a climate of trust will be created between management and workers.

Disadvantages

This type of leadership style could lead to deviant behavior simply because management takes a "hands-off" approach. Employees might start to do less work because lack of supervision makes it easy to do so. In other words, "the mice will play when the cat is away."

Paternalistic

It is likely that this type of leadership style will become less prevalent in the future. Work-life balance will increase in importance, and that means employees will increasingly want to separate their work lives from their personal lives. Some organizations will find paternalistic leadership beneficial, but the style will diminish as a whole.

Advantages

There will always be employees who want management to serve a dual role as boss and parent. For those individuals, paternalistic leadership style works best.

Disadvantages

The style of leadership will have no value to global organizations because paternalistic leaders value employee relationships that are personal and professional...and this is simply not possible in a worldwide operation. It will also have no value to organizations that promote telecommuting because the personal element is missing.

Transactional

This leadership style will have a place in the future due to its simplicity. Organizational leaders who wear many hats will use it so they have time to focus on other important workplace aspects. A small business owner is an example of this type of leader.

Advantages

Rewards typically motivate people, and they will continue to do so in the future. Most employees have monetary needs, and transactional leaders provide for those needs. Money has always been important to people, and that will not change in the future.

Disadvantages

Money is an advantageous aspect of transactional leadership, but it also has a downside due to its limitations. Money alone cannot make an employee happy, and that will not change in the future.

Transformational

Politicians have shown that charisma is important for leadership. It influences people, alters mindsets, and leads to change in organizations. For these reasons, the transformational leadership style will be alive and well in the future.

Advantages

Increased competition will force many organizations to operate in a crisis mode, and this is where transformational leaders are at their best. Positive thinking is critical for troubled organizations, and transformational leadership helps achieve it.

Disadvantages

Transformational leaders are not always honest, and this can create trust issues with employees. If these leaders choose to ignore the reality of situations, their style will not be successful in the future.

Summary

Leaders have a major bearing on the way organizations function. They make decisions that impact workplaces by implementing procedures, establishing structure, dictating change, and shaping culture.

Their decisions are based on a variety of factors, but they are always influenced by their leadership styles.

This book focuses on the present and future of leadership style in organizations. Specifically, it examines the style of authoritarian leaders, democratic leaders, laissez-faire leaders, paternalistic leaders, transactional leaders, and transformational leaders. Workplace examples are used throughout for illustration and clarification, and this makes learning easier and more enjoyable for the reader.

Congratulations! You now understand leadership style...an important aspect of organizational behavior.

Toxic Leadership

Introduction

The term "toxic leader" was originally established by Marcia Whicker in the mid-1990s to describe leaders that failed miserably in their positions at the top. She described these individuals as selfish, deceitful, controlling, and non-productive. Many of them had successful careers, but that success came at the expense of others.

Over the years, other people have written about toxic leadership. They expanded upon Whicker's work using well-known examples...and the Wall Street scandals of the not so distant past gave them a lot to write about. As might be expected, all of these writers agreed that toxic leadership is bad for employees and organizations.

This book provides a broad overview of toxic leadership. It examines the characteristics that make up these leaders, the tools they use to maintain their positions, and the effects that their actions have on workplaces. It also suggests ways to survive working in an organization with toxic leadership.

Toxic leadership occurs when leaders abuse the relationships they have with employees and others associated with the organization. These individuals are often aware of their actions, but they simply do not care about the damage they do to others because their only concern is personal advancement.

Please consider the following example of toxic leadership:

> Salvatore takes over as the CEO of a publicly traded computer hardware manufacturing company. The company is surviving, but it has not been profitable for a few years, and the stockholders are demanding better performance.
>
> Within six months of taking over the organization, Salvatore lays off ten percent of the management staff because he claims the company is top heavy. He also eliminates 15 percent of the manufacturing jobs after his analysis determines that the production plants are overstaffed.
>
> These cuts save the company over 15 million dollars a year. Profitability returns, and the stock price increases 25 percent. This looks good for Salvatore, and he is rewarded with a three million dollar bonus at the end of the fiscal year.
>
> However, 18 months later, the company starts to lose money again. The stock price goes below its value before Salvatore took over as CEO, and the stockholders are furious. Salvatore is terminated from his a position with a two million dollar severance package.
>
> In short, Salvatore was paid over 5 million dollars to reduce the market value of the computer hardware company. He profited while employees lost jobs and the company faltered.

The above example is not a true story, but it is indicative of the fallout from toxic leadership. Typically, these individuals leave an organization in worse condition than it was when they took over the top management position. Sometimes the damage they do is so severe that companies are forced to shut down.

Now that have some basic understanding of toxic leadership and have seen an example, let's move to a discussion on specific characteristics of these individuals.

Characteristics

Toxic leaders have definitive characteristics associated with them. Certain traits, such as being competitive in their style of management, produce some positive effects in workplaces. However, most toxic leader characteristics negatively impact employees and organizations.

In general, toxic leaders are:

Autocratic

Toxic leaders essentially are in a style of management all by itself. They do not fall into the traditional leadership categories that consist of authoritarian, democratic, laissez-faire, paternalistic, transactional, and transformational. However, they have some traits in common with autocratic leaders because they:

- Act as a dictator in the sense that they use fear to establish power
- Communicate from top to bottom with limited communication in the reverse direction
- Focus on control and maintain close supervision so they do not lose control
- View other types of leadership style (such as democratic) as inefficient because control is limited

Unlikeable

Toxic leaders are in control of their employees, but this does not mean they are liked by those employees. In fact, workers typically dislike toxic leaders because:

- They are afraid to argue or question decisions due to the fear of jeopardizing their jobs.
- Their creativity and diversity are stifled.
- They are not entitled to opinions, and there is no room for debate or disagreement.
- There is only one right answer...and it comes from the toxic leader.

Untrustable

Trust builds relationships, and lack of trust deteriorates them. Since toxic leaders do whatever is necessary to accomplish their goals, they often violate the trust of their employees. Those employees then lose their commitment to their organization because they no longer identify with its values....and the workplace begins to spiral downward.

The worst part about a loss of trust is that once it is gone, it is difficult to restore. However, many toxic leaders are not concerned with getting that trust back as long as they have achieved their personal goals.

Arrogant

Arrogance comes naturally to many individuals. In workplaces, some employees do not even realize they are displaying arrogance because they are unaware of their behavior. They are trying to do their job to the best of their ability, and they unintentional display conceitedness or superiority.

Arrogance is acceptable for some employees, but it produces problems for leaders because they create a barrier between themselves and their employees. That barrier prevents the flow of communication and restricts the exchange of ideas and information.

Many toxic leaders are arrogant. They often realize their arrogance, but they simply do not care. They have an agenda that is going to move forward regardless of who is upset or offended. Unfortunately, that agenda is about personal gain rather than organizational growth and prosperity.

Competitive

Competition is good for organizations. It makes sense because the best positions are often very lucrative, and employees work hard to attain those positions. In short, they compete with each other to reach the top.

Toxic managers push competition to another level. They are over competitive and will do whatever they need to do to get to the top. This is not good because dishonest and unethical activities are often part of their game plan. Competent people get passed over for positions because rules are bent or broken, and this prevents the best employees from rising to the top. Ultimately, the organization suffers...and so do the employees within it.

Micromanagers

As noted in the introduction, toxic leaders are controlling because they need to make sure their agenda is moving forward. One method used to ensure control is micromanagement.

In the case of a CEO, the employees most often micromanaged are top-ranking executives. These executives then lose their motivation to work hard, and the negativity slowly trickles down into the rank and file employees.

Micromanaging is not good for an organization at any level. If the CEO is guilty of this type of management style, then it is only a matter of time before the entire workforce culture is impacted.

Bullies

Some people might find it difficult to believe that top leaders of organizations are bullies. After all, these individuals have reached positions where their word is the law, and they should not have to coerce others to behave in desired ways. In many cases, this is true...but not if the top person is a toxic leader.

Toxic leaders rise to their positions by intimidating and mistreating others, and they have no intention of changing their tactics. In fact, once they reach the top they believe they are even more justified to bully others simply because they are the top authority. Bullying also prevents rivals and dissenters from becoming threats and helps toxic leaders maintain their position of dominance.

Inflexible

Good leaders know that they need to be flexible in order to adapt when it is best for their organization. Toxic leaders view flexibility as a sign of weakness and instead choose to remain firm in their decisions...regardless of whether they are right or wrong.

Inflexibility is another tactic used by toxic leaders to prevent dissenting employees from becoming threats to their power. When workers realize that their leaders will not change their minds under any circumstances, they stop opposing them because that opposition is pointless.

Insecure

Confidence is an important trait for leaders. Employees expect those in charge to be confident, and leaders who fail to live up to that expectation lose the respect of the workforce. This is not a problem for most good leaders because they are competent individuals who have worked hard to achieve their position. They understand their job responsibilities and the employees in their workplace, and this leads to happy workers and organizational success.

Toxic leaders do not fit into the good leader category, but they attempt to imitate them by portraying a high level of self-confidence. Some are successful in this portrayal, and it leads to the illusion that they are competent. Others fail to create that illusion...and their insecurity is quite transparent.

In theory, insecurity should be an expected trait of toxic leaders. After all, these individuals reach their positions through deceitful rather than honest behavior...so why would anyone expect them to be competent or confident?

Narcissistic

Narcissistic people are self-absorbed. They admire themselves over everyone else, and their ego controls many aspects of their behavior. Based on this, it is rather easy to see why toxic managers are narcissistic because they value themselves over all other employees. Worse yet, they view themselves as more important than the organization they are responsible for overseeing...and this is never good.

In regard to narcissism, always remember the following:

Narcissistic employees can damage organizations...but narcissistic leaders can destroy them.

Discriminatory

As more businesses compete in the global marketplace, diversity becomes increasingly important. Good leaders understand this point and diversify their employees. They establish heterogeneous workforces that stimulate creativity and innovation during problem-solving. They want the synergy that evolves from different minds.

Toxic leaders do not value diversity and would rather discriminate. They prefer people like themselves so they can further their agenda...which is to benefit personally from the organization that they oversee. Workforces under toxic leadership are not creative and innovative, but this is not a concern for the leaders because they typically make important decisions themselves.

Condescending

Toxic leaders are often critical. They tear employees down rather than build them up because criticism maintains control while praise leads to the empowerment that breeds independent thinking. This is why so many toxic leaders exhibit condescending characteristics.

The following are some organizational examples of how toxic leaders display their associated characteristics in the workplace:

Organizational example #1

Victoria owns a bakery. When she makes business decisions, she does not trust or consult anyone else. She makes choices based on her perception of the situation, and she is not open to people who challenge her decisions.

There are problems associated with Victoria's leadership style. She has made some decisions that her managers knew were wrong, but they did not challenge her due to the fear of retribution. They know Victoria does not take kindly to disagreement or criticism, and she does not allow people to debate her choices. This is demoralizing to Victoria's managers because they feel like they have no freedom and their opinions do not matter. It has also resulted in some costly mistakes that could have been prevented with some discussion.

Victoria's toxic leadership style is such that she is inflexible and does not trust others to help her make decisions. Her tight control suppresses the individuality of her managers, negatively impacts their moral, and prevents them from engaging in healthy debate.

Organizational example #2

Mark is the CEO of a pest control company owned by venture capitalists. His organization services retail establishments in 21 different states. The hierarchical structure of the company consists of a CEO, two vice presidents, one general manager, one office manager, ten office workers, 24 area managers, and 380 licensed pesticide applicators.

Mark does not let any management employees approach the venture capitalist owners with suggestions or ideas for improving the company. He makes it clear that he is the only person who is allowed to talk to these individuals, and there will be consequences if anyone goes over his head. This demoralizes Mark's managers and causes them to dislike him as a boss.

Mark's micromanagement is based on his concern that he might not receive credit for an idea generated by someone else in the company. His toxic leadership style shows his insecurity and demotivates his workforce.

Organizational example #3

Tonya is the president of an office equipment distribution company. She decides to establish a team of employees to find ways to lower shipping costs. The team consists of the office manager, purchasing manager, safety manager, quality manager, inventory control manager, and shipping manager. Tonya chose these individuals based on their skill levels and areas of expertise, but she is not confident that they will make the right cost-cutting decisions for the organization. She believes she knows best what needs to be done, so she monitors their activities closely and makes sure she has the final say on any decisions made by the group.

The team comes up with three new cost-cutting ideas, but Tonya rejects them all. She tells them their ideas make no sense, and she lets them know that she expects better ideas from them as a group. She states that they have embarrassed themselves and the company, and this is not acceptable. The team wants to abandon the project, but they meet again because Tonya requires them to do so.

Tonya is a micromanager, and her critical comments demotivate the team members. They know that regardless of their findings, Tonya will react in a condescending manner and override their ideas because she believes she knows best. Tonya truly is a toxic leader.

Now that you understand some of the characteristics of toxic leaders, let move into the tools they use to control others and personally benefit.

Tools

Toxic leaders use specific tools for their jobs. Unfortunately, these tools are mostly used to maintain control over employees rather than to make organizations grow and prosper.

The toxic leader's tools include:

Power

Most leaders control people's decision making power for the benefit of their organization, but toxic leaders use this tool for personal gain. They make decisions that affect their control of the organization, and they appoint "puppets" to make less critical decisions. Please consider the following example:

> Gertrude is a toxic leader. She runs her organization with an iron fist and will not allow employees to make decisions without her approval. She does this to maintain strict control over all aspects of the workplace.
>
> Gertrude needs a marketing manager to replace the one she recently terminated. There are several qualified candidates in the marketing department, but none of them are people that Gertrude wants in charge. Instead, she chooses a production supervisor named Arthur for the job. Arthur knows very little about marketing, but this does not concern Gertrude because he is a "yes man" who will only make decisions that help her maintain control of the organization.

In the above example, Gertrude arranges the decision making power structure for her own personal gain. She is only looking out for herself, and there is nothing beneficial for the organization or employees.

Games

This tool utilizes mind games. It is a form of bullying where potential rivals or dissenters are assigned tasks that they cannot possibly complete. Please consider the following example:

> Ronald is a toxic leader who sees Janet, the human resources director, as a potential threat to his control of other employees. In a well-planned move, he puts Janet in charge of a construction project. He tells her that she is a skilled employee who can handle the task.
>
> Unfortunately, Janet has no engineering, building, or architectural experience. Ronald knows this and purposely assigns her to the task because he knows that she will not be able to complete it.

In the above example, Ronald is setting up Janet to fail so she will not be considered for other opportunities.

Discipline

Toxic leaders look for rule violations to discipline people they do not like or do not want to see advance. Please consider the following example:

> Leslie is a toxic leader who views Mitch, the director of finance, as a threat to her control and authority. Leslie knows that Mitch has been using his company vehicle for personal use, so she disciplines him with an unpaid suspension.
>
> Mitch's personal use of his company vehicle is technically a violation of company policy. However, other managers do this on a regular basis without facing any disciplinary action.

In the above example, Leslie appears to be adhering to company policy rather than singling out a rival or dissenter. However, the reality is that she wants to punish Mitch to make him look bad.

Status

This involves the power to control work-related privileges that symbolize authority. Executive parking lots, private bathrooms, and catered lunches are examples of status tools that many leaders have at their disposal. Toxic leaders remove these privileges from individuals that they consider to be a threat, and this is demeaning. Please consider the following example:

> Patrick is a toxic leader. He considers the vice-president of production Mary to be a threat to his control. He wants Mary to leave the organization, so he removes some of her perks. Specifically, he takes away her parking space in the covered garage and announces that all production employees must park in the manufacturing plant lot for security reasons.
>
> In reality, Patrick sees no legitimate security reason for all production employees to park in the manufacturing plant lot. He implements this rule because he wants to discourage Mary so she will leave the organization.

In the above example, Mary lost a privilege. On the surface, this might not seem significant. However, privileges indicate status and achievement and are therefore important to employees.

Structure

This refers to the structure of work relationships in the organization. Employees have certain likes and dislikes when it comes to coworkers, and this causes them to prefer working with some people more than others.

Toxic managers use this tool to monitor or control employee work relationships for their own personal gain. Please consider the following example:

> Larry is a toxic leader. He is insecure about his position and constantly monitors his employees to eliminate potential threats to his authority and control.
>
> Rhonda is one of Larry's favorite managers. She does whatever he asks, and keeps him informed of workplace happenings. Larry knows that Rhonda supports him, and he uses her for many of his undermining activities. Rhonda is not liked by many of her coworkers, but this is fine with Larry as long as she feeds him information.
>
> Larry is suspicious that the office personnel might be plotting against him behind his back. Since he is not always around them, he moves Rhonda's desk into the office to monitor their conversations and report back to him. The office employees are not happy about this move, but they cannot stop it.

In the above example, Rhonda has no reason for her desk to be in the office other than the fact that she can be a snitch for Larry. In this sense, Larry uses the structure tool to maintain his control as a toxic leader.

Now that you understanding of some of the tools used by toxic leaders, let's move into the effects that their actions have on workplaces.

Effects

Toxic leadership has a variety of different effects on employees and organizations. Unfortunately, almost all of those effects are negative, and some of the major ones are listed below.

Trust

Toxic leaders almost always violate trust because they destroy workplaces while furthering their own agenda. Unfortunately, this lack of trust often goes beyond the toxic leader. Many workers lose trust in the organization as a whole...even after the toxic leader is no longer a part of it.

As was noted in the characteristics section, the worst part about lost trust is the fact that it is very difficult to restore. Good leaders realize this and work toward being sincere and honest so their employees have faith in their actions.

Turnover

Once employees have had enough of toxic leadership, they look for employment elsewhere. This means good employees are lost because toxic leaders are only interested in furthering their own agenda. In certain situations, the exiting of workers is welcomed by toxic leaders...but it is rarely welcomed by other employees who care about their organizations.

Commitment

Commitment is the feeling employees have toward achieving the goals of the organization. Employees who work under toxic leadership lose faith that their leaders will do the right thing, and they are no longer committed to the organization. Without employee commitment, organizations cannot be successful, and their survival is at stake.

In short, employee commitment is critical for organizational growth and prosperity...and that commitment diminishes under toxic leadership.

Motivation

This effect is a no-brainer. Employees who work under toxic leadership lose motivation due to the fact that their leaders only care about themselves. If bosses do not care about employees, then employees do not care about their organization...and they are not motivated to perform their jobs to the best of their ability. This creates a lose/lose situation for the employer and the employee...with the only winner being the toxic leader.

Fear

Control is a very high priority for toxic leaders. In fact, often times it is the most important aspect of the job for some of these individuals. Based on this importance, toxic leaders prefer to rule by fear because fear maintains control. Employees who experience fear are afraid to speak out against the leader due to the consequences that might prevail.

Stress

Toxic leaders create stress throughout the workplace. Part of this is planned because it helps them establish authority and maintain control. However, stress is hard on employees and can lead to physical or mental health issues. Unfortunately, toxic leaders are not concerned with employee health as long as they benefit personally.

Now you understand some of the major effects of toxic leadership, and it is rather obvious that they are all bad. However, this raises a question. If toxic leadership has all negative effects, how can employees tolerate it and work under such conditions? The next section answers that question by discussing methods of employee survival.

Surviving

This section suggests methods for combating toxic leadership and surviving the fallout. These methods include:

Control

Employees need to maintain control by not reacting emotionally to the negative actions of toxic leaders. Sometimes these leaders are looking for angry outbursts so they can implement termination policies that get rid of the offending employees permanently.

Emotional control also prevents mental and physical health issues that can result from extreme emotional reactions. Regardless of the harm done to health, employees need to react appropriately to avoid further complication of the situation.

Patience

This is similar to the control method because employees need to think before they react to the situation. Patience allows for the rational reactions that are necessary to deal with an assault from a toxic leader, and employees can gather their thoughts so they can combat the toxic leader with facts.

Typically, patience works well for employees because they have time to build cases against toxic leaders. Strong cases have a good chance of stopping this type of behavior because the toxic leaders' negative actions are exposed on a repeated basis.

Collaboration

Employees need to work together to combat toxic leadership. Rarely do "lone wolves" survive because they do not have enough power to combat leadership. However, there is strength in numbers. Collaboration with coworkers builds the necessary power to fight toxic leaders, and employees are more confident in their responses.

Collaboration is about synergy, and synergy is important for establishing strategies to combat toxic leadership. Employees can use all of the negative behavior they have witnessed to build successful cases against toxic leaders.

Summary

Toxic leaders care about themselves far more than they do about the organizations they oversee. They value control above everything else, and they use their power to maintain that control. They are not concerned about the damage they inflict on employees or workplaces as long as they personally benefit from the situation.

This book provides a broad overview of toxic leadership. It examines characteristics that make up these leaders, the tools they use to maintain their positions, and the effects that their actions have on workplaces. It also suggests ways to survive working in an organization with toxic leadership.

Congratulations! You now understand more about toxic leadership....and important aspect of organizational behavior.

Micromanagement

	Page Number
Introduction	29
Focused	29
Decision oriented	29
Self-absorbed	29
Causes	30
Justifiable micromanagement	30
Unjustifiable micromanagement	31
Insecurity	32
Change	32
Loss of control	32
Loss of connection	33
Lack of experience	33
Lack of competence	33
Lack of trust	33
Inability to delegate	33
Loss of recognition	33
Effects	34
Productivity	34
Motivation	34
Empowerment	34
Turnover	34
Potential	34
Creativity	35
Innovation	35
Collaboration	35
Workload	35
Surviving	29
Observe	36
Learn	36
Achieve	36
Adhere	37
Inform	37
Promote	37

Introduction

It is important to begin with a definition. For this book, micromanagement is defined as:

Managers who devote unnecessary attention to minor details

Micromanagers exist in organizations of every type and size. Their jobs differ, but they share common traits while performing those jobs. In general, these individuals are:

Focused

They focus intently on the aspects of their jobs that they consider important. Unfortunately for their subordinates, this means focusing on every detail of processes and procedures...which often hinders productivity. An example is as follows:

> Jennifer works at a flower shop. Her main job is to assemble custom floral arrangements for special events. However, the owner Thomas slows her down considerably. Thomas insists on looking at every flower before Jennifer uses it. If he is not in the shop, then she cannot assemble the arrangements.
>
> Thomas is very focused on making sure every flower meets his specifications before it is used. However, instead of conveying his specifications to Jennifer for her decision making, he micromanages and examines every flower himself.

In this example, Thomas is a micromanager because he does not see the big picture. Instead, he focuses on the smaller aspects of Jennifer's job responsibilities.

Decision-oriented

Micromanagers are strong decision makers. Because of this, they often have difficulty delegating and become upset when their subordinates make a decision without their approval.

Micromanagers' decisions are usually well thought since they are capable individuals who understand the needs of the organization. However, the downside of their decision making is that it is counter-productive. Many times subordinates are perfectly capable of making decisions, but they are not allowed to do so by micromanaging bosses. This delays tasks from getting completed, hinders organizational efficiency, and prevents goals and objectives from being accomplished.

Self-absorbed

It is not uncommon for micromanagers to be self-absorbed. In other words, they only show concern for their own thoughts and ideas. They have been known to be:

Narcissistic

They believe their ideas, methods, decisions, and thoughts are the best...and this is why they should be in control of every aspect of job tasks.

Overbearing

Most people who have been micromanaged understand that these types of managers can be overbearing. Their dominant and controlling presence has the potential to upset any employee...regardless of that employee's talent or disposition.

Unaware

This is the most interesting trait. Many individuals report having worked for a micromanager...but very few people admit to being one. This indicates that micromanagers truly are unaware of their actions.

Micromanagers often fail to realize they are controlling, narcissistic, overbearing, and domineering. They deny micromanaging, and instead claim that they are organized and conscientious...and they are only doing what is best for the organization

In short, micromanagers provide some good for organizations because they prevent mistakes by making sure their employees adhere to specific details of work-related tasks. However, for the most part, micromanagers hinder productivity be monitoring processes and procedures far too closely. They have been compared to bullies due to the high level of control that they possess...and their refusal or inability to delegate or relinquish that control.

Now that you have a basic understanding of micromanaging, let's move on to the causes of people's micromanagement.

Causes

This section focuses on the causes of micromanagement. In other words, it examines some of the reasons people micromanage others.

Micromanagement is typically not good. However, contrary to what some people might think, some situations legitimize this style of management. Below are examples of workplace situations that cause managers to micromanage their subordinates. Some of these examples justify the micromanagement, while others do not.

Justifiable micromanagement

The following are examples of justifiable micromanagement in workplaces:

Example #1

John works in inventory control for an office supply distributor. This is his first week on the job, and his boss Nancy makes sure that every aspect of his work is correct. She reviews all of his computer work and monitors his actions while he is doing his job. She also tells him to come to her with any questions so she can decide the proper way to proceed...and he can learn proper company procedure in the process.

Nancy is a micromanager. She watches John closely, checks his work, and makes decisions for him. However, John is a new employee, and he might make mistakes that are costly for the organization. In this situation, Nancy's micromanagement is justifiable because it is based on John's lack of experience.

Example #2

Vicki works as a nurse at a doctor's office and has made several mistakes in the past few weeks. Dr. DeLong is concerned about her performance, so he starts to monitor her work more closely. He watches her take patients' blood pressure and listens to her conversations with them. He also tells her to not answer specific questions regarding medical treatment until she consults with him.

Dr. DeLong is a micromanager. He watches Vicki closely as she performs her job, and he does not allow her to make medical treatment decisions without his approval. In this situation, Dr. DeLong's micromanagement is justified because it is based on the mistakes that Vicki has made in the recent past.

Unjustifiable micromanagement

The following are examples of unjustifiable micromanagement in workplaces:

Example #1

Charles is a supervisor who has established a team of employees to find ways to lower costs at a toy manufacturer. He chose these employees based on their skill levels and areas of expertise, but he is not confident that they will make the right cost-cutting decisions for the organization. He believes he knows best what needs to be done, so he monitors their activities closely and makes sure he has the final say on any decisions made by the group.

Charles is a micromanager. He watches his team very closely and does not allow decisions to be made without his approval because he does not believe the members will make the best choices for the toy manufacturer. In this situation, Charles micromanagement is not justified because it is based on his lack of trust in the team members.

Example #2

Shianne manages three employees in the quality department of a stamping plant. She monitors her workers' actions closely because she feels she needs to have control over all aspects of her department.

Shianne's employees are irritated by her behavior, and they have told her that she does not need to watch their every move. However, she claims her monitoring is necessary due to her conscientiousness and the fact that she cares about the work put out by her department.

Shianne is a micromanager. She watches her employees very closely, and they find this unnecessary and annoying. In this situation, Shianne's micromanagement is unjustified because it is based on her inability to delegate.

Example #3

Jerome supervises four workers in the safety department of a car rental company. He will not let his workers approach upper management with any suggestion for safety improvements...he makes it clear that he is the only person who is allowed to make these suggestions. His employees do not understand his reasoning for doing this, but they comply because he is their boss.

Jerome is a micromanager. He will not let his employees talk to upper management about safety ideas that they think would benefit the car rental company. In this situation, Jerome's micromanagement is unjustified because it is based on his concern that he might not receive credit for an idea generated by his department.

Based on the above examples, micromanaging does have a place in organizations. However, that place is limited to certain situations...and some people fail to realize those situations. That being said, the following are specific causes of micromanagement in organizations:

Insecurity

Sometimes micromanagement occurs because supervisors believe they have less knowledge than their subordinates. This might seem strange at first glance, but insecurity creates the need for supervisors to control employees to avoid being overshadowed by them.

Unfortunately, this type of supervisor behavior has consequences because people are held back from performing at optimum levels....which impacts productivity. It is rather obvious that this type of micromanagement is unjustified.

Change

Employees going through change are often unsure of how to perform their jobs. For example, a company might be bought by another organization, and employees are uncertain about the most important aspects of their jobs. In this type of situation, micromanaging is justified so employees can be helped to do the right things during every step of a process or procedure. In fact, some employees prefer to be micromanaged after a merger or takeover.

Loss of control

Some supervisors need to micromanage their employees due to their fear of losing control of them. These bosses put tight reins on their workers to prevent them from straying off in different directions and making decisions on their own. In this situation, micromanagement is unjustified because it is based on fear.

Loss of connection

Some supervisors feel themselves drifting away from their employees. They lose understanding of the day-to-day operations and can no longer relate to the jobs of the people they oversee. This is difficult for some bosses...especially if they were well connected at one time.

One way for supervisors to reconnect with workers is to micromanage them. This keeps them involved in their subordinates work because they monitor their everyday actions.

Unfortunately, the loss of freedom that results from reconnection can be painful for employees. In this situation, micromanagement is unjustified because it serves no real purpose in terms of benefitting the organization.

Lack of experience

Supervisors sometimes micromanage their employees when those employees lack the necessary experience to make decisions independently. Please refer to justifiable micromanagement example #1 above for an example of this cause.

Lack of competence

Incompetent subordinates often need to be micromanaged in order to properly complete their assigned job tasks. Please refer to justifiable micromanagement example #2 above for an example of this cause.

Lack of trust

Some supervisors micromanage their employees because they do not trust them to properly complete tasks. Please refer to unjustifiable micromanagement example #1 above for an example of this cause.

Inability to delegate

Supervisors who cannot or refuse to delegate tasks often micromanage their employees. Please refer to unjustifiable micromanagement example #2 above for an example of this cause.

Loss of recognition

Supervisors who are afraid they will not be recognized for their employees' work often resort to micromanaging them. Please refer to unjustifiable micromanagement example #3 above for an example of this cause.

Now that you are aware of some of the causes of micromanagement, let's move to the next section that discusses the effects of this style of management.

Effects

The most significant aspect of a discussion on micromanaging involves the effects it has on workplaces. This knowledge is critical because it gives a good indication of whether this management style should be tolerated or eliminated. That being said, the following are factors affected by micromanagement in organizations:

Productivity

Employees become less productive when they are micromanaged. This is because they are spending less time doing actual work, and they are spending more time waiting for their supervisors to approve every task they complete.

Supervisors who are heavy micromanagers can literally bring productivity to a halt as employees wait in line for approval. It is similar to a man waiting to see a doctor at her office. If the doctor spends an extra 15 minutes with each of the three patients ahead of the man, then he will need to wait an additional 45 minutes to see her. Based on this, it is relatively easy to see how micromanaging can have a major effect on productivity.

Motivation

Micromanaged employees lose motivation due to the restrictions placed on them by their supervisors. When employees are not motivated, they do not perform to the best of their abilities. Lack of performance affects the bottom line because organizational efficiency suffers.

Empowerment

Empowered employees are more involved employees because they take ownership of their jobs. Micromanaged employees are not able to take ownership of their jobs. They are not empowered because their bosses dictate their actions and make decisions for them. This is not good for the employees or organizations.

Turnover

Employees who are not able to make decisions in their jobs often become frustrated. If that frustration continues for prolonged periods, those employees begin to look for other positions where they can make decisions. In this sense, micromanagement prevents employees from finding job satisfaction, and that lack of job satisfaction leads to turnover.

Potential

This is one of the most serious and often overlooked effects of micromanaging. Employees who are micromanaged are prevented from learning new skills due to the controls imposed on them. Consequently, they never reach their potential for growth in organizations, and this is bad for employees and employers.

Creativity

Many people think that creativity is limited to artists, musicians, designers, and similar job descriptions. However, this is not true because creativity comes in many shapes and sizes. For example, an accountant can be creative by coming up with a new way to track costs for a meat processing plant. All the accountant needs is the freedom to experiment with different ideas....and then creativity begins to flow.

Micromanagers restrict their employees' freedom and prevent them from being creative. When this happens, organizations lose the potential for novel thinking that could make processes and procedures better, less expensive, or more efficient.

Innovation

Similar to creativity, innovation also requires freedom. When employees are micromanaged, that freedom comes with a very short leash that prevents them from using original thinking to come up with new ideas. Once again, organizations lose opportunities to get better.

Another interesting note about micromanagement and innovation involves secrecy. Micromanaged employees are not likely to share original ideas with their bosses because they fear their bosses will take the credit for those ideas. This makes sense because micromanagers have to approve every decision made by a subordinate...so they decide if, how, and when that idea will be released to people in higher positions.

Collaboration

Workplace collaboration is the sharing of thoughts and ideas between coworkers. Micromanaged employees are led every step of the way, and their thinking is not shared with others unless they are told to do so by their supervisor. This puts collaboration at a standstill, and it does little to help organizations grow and prosper.

Workload

This factor pertains to the supervisors doing the micromanaging. These individuals create a lot more work for themselves when they oversee every detail of their employees' jobs. At some point, this workload will become unbearable and stress will result. That stress is not good for supervisors, employees, or the organization.

Excessive workload is a good reason why supervisors should do a serious self-analysis of their management style to determine if they are micromanagers. This analysis could prevent a lot of unnecessary grief and aggravation.

Now you understand some of the major negative effects of micromanaging. So, what does this mean? It means that employees experiencing this type of management style need to learn how to tolerate it and prevent it from getting worse. Prevention is discussed later in this book, and survival is discussed in the next section.

Surviving

It is now rather obvious that micromanaging is usually not good for employees or organizations. However, supervisors have micromanaged in the past, they do it today, and they will do it in the future. That being said, there needs to be a way to deal with these controlling individuals. This is not easy, but it is possible...and it is also essential for survival.

The following are techniques for surviving micromanaging supervisors:

Observe

Employees need to be observant of workplace happenings. For example, if it is apparent that cost-cutting measures are a priority, then workers should prepare cost-cutting measures for their jobs that can be presented to their bosses upon request. This is important for several reasons including:

- It shows employees have initiative.
- It indicates employees have an understanding of the needs of the organization.
- It builds supervisor confidence in employees.
- It eliminates the need for excessive micromanagement since the tasks are regularly being completed.
- It builds solid supervisor-subordinate relationships.

In short, a little observation goes a long way...all it takes is some time and effort.

Learn

Like it or not, politics play a role in virtually every organization. This technique involves politicking where employees learn what their bosses like so they can cater to their preferences. To do this, questions need to be asked by employees. Do their bosses like humor, sports, theater, cards, old cars, music, or movies? Understanding their preferences helps build better supervisor/subordinate relationships. Whatever is done, workers need to refrain from doing things that agitate their bosses because this will have the opposite effect.

Achieve

This involves staying ahead of the game, and it works well as a survival technique. Supervisors become micromanagers because they require their subordinates to perform job tasks accurately and correctly. The employees who consistently achieve this requirement are given the least attention by the supervisor...which means they are monitored less closely.

This technique will not completely prevent supervisors from micromanaging because their nature is to monitor people closely. However, it will make them less controlling and overbearing....and that is very important for employee survival.

Adhere

This is a common-sense suggestion for surviving micromanagement. Employees should always follow the rules established by organizations. This might not always help build better supervisor/subordinate relationships, but employees who do not follow rules can expect the opposite effect...and they can also expect to be micromanaged even closer.

Inform

This involves keeping supervisors updated. Micromanagers do not like when they are unable to answer questions about the teams or departments that they are overseeing, and employees can help prevent this by providing them with information. This survival technique is similar to the achieve technique because it results in supervisors being less controlling and overbearing.

Promote

Employees need to promote the fact that they trust their supervisors and appreciate their support. Once again, this improves employee/supervisor relationships and results in supervisors reducing their level of control.

Discuss

This technique works because many supervisors do not realize that they are micromanagers. Employees need to let their supervisors know that they trust them and value their opinions, but they would like to do some things more independently. This can be done on a trial basis if the supervisors are uncomfortable, but the point is for employees to discuss their need for independence in order to get their micromanaging supervisors to relinquish some of their control.

Now you are aware of some techniques for surviving a micromanaging boss. While these are significant, it is even more important to prevent micromanagement in organizations so the negative effects do not have a chance to take root. Ways of doing this are discussed in the next section.

Preventing

It is great that there are ways to survive micromanaging, but survival techniques treat the symptoms instead of the root cause. Leaders of organizations need to find ways to prevent their supervisors from becoming micromanagers so the associated pitfalls do not have a chance to occur.

Suggestions for doing this include:

Hire effectively

Organizations need to screen people they interview for signs of micromanagement. This might seem difficult, but it is possible. For example, the following five questions can indicate the potential for a supervisor candidate to micromanage:

- Ideally, how would a team that you are in charge of accomplish goals and objectives?
- In general, how do you feel about employees making decisions without their supervisors?
- How do you feel about delegating authority to employees in your department?
- How much information do you provide your employees with when they need to complete a job-related task?
- Do you consider yourself a detail-oriented manager? Please explain the reasoning for your answer.

The answers to these questions can provide a lot about a person's tendency to micromanage. More interestingly, true micromanagers usually do not realize they are giving themselves up as being controlling and overbearing because they do not view themselves in this manner.

Communicate expectations

Make it clear that all employees in the organization are expected to make decisions and be held accountable for their decisions. This gives workers decision making power and shows supervisors that micromanagement is not needed or wanted.

Encourage collaboration

Encourage employees to work together to find solutions. This prevents them from going to their supervisor for every decision.

Collaboration also brings multiple minds together for more diverse problem resolution. This increases workers' confidence while inspiring creativity and innovation. The end result is a win-win situation for employees and the organization.

Accept mistakes

Make it clear that mistakes are going to happen, and those mistakes are acceptable as long as employees strive to correct the associated problems and prevent a reoccurrence. This encourages employees to think on their own and not rely on their supervisors for every decision.

Mistake acceptance also prevents supervisors from micromanaging because their efforts to prevent every error are unnecessary. Employee blunders do not reflect negativity on bosses because those mistakes are expected to occur.

Summary

Micromanagers are present in organizations all over the world. Often times these individuals mean well, and there are some benefits to their management style. However, they also create workplace problems, and their actions hinder the growth of employees and organizations.

This book focuses on micromanaging in organizations. First, it explores causes of micromanagement including insecurity, change, loss of control, loss of connection, lack of experience, lack of competence, lack of trust, inability to delegate, and loss of recognition. Next, it examines the way micromanaging affects productivity, motivation, empowerment, turnover, potential, creativity, innovation, collaboration, and workload. Then it looks at methods for surviving a micromanaging supervisor that include being able to observe, learn, achieve, adhere, inform, promote, and discuss. Finally, it offers suggestions for preventing micromanagement that require organizations to hire effectively, communicate expectations, encourage collaboration, and accept mistakes.

Congratulations! You now understand more about micromanaging...an important aspect of organizational behavior.

Organizational Culture

Introduction to culture

Every organization has unique experiences, philosophies, behaviors, norms, and values. They also have specific methods and patterns for interacting with suppliers, customers, employees, and the community. When combined, these attributes define an organization and make up its culture.

Culture starts at the top of an organization and works its way down into the rank and file. Employees can help establish behaviors and norms, but they do not have the same power as those in the upper levels of the established hierarchy. Top ranking members are the only people who have the authority, influence, and control needed to create the overall culture of the organization.

In companies, culture provides guidelines for productivity, performance, service, and quality. It applies to everyone and can be difficult to alter without solid planning.

In short, every culture is distinctive based on the characteristics of the organization. Culture describes an organization and explains its purpose in society. It is also created by the most influential members, establishes policies and procedures, and can be challenging to change without a plan.

Now let's move into a discussion on the ways that culture affects the actions of people in organizations.

Relationship of culture

Organizational culture is associated with many different aspects of organizational behavior. These associations influence employee actions and establish a perception of the organization. Let's take a closer look at these relationships and their impact:

Decision making

Effective decision making is critical for the survival of an organization, and that decision making is almost always influenced by culture. Employees think about their organization's norms and values before deciding the direction to proceed. If they go against those norms and values, they risk bringing about change that might be resisted by coworkers or rejected by higher management.

Let's look at the entire decision-making process and examine how culture plays a role throughout. First, the problem needs to be identified so people can think about potential solutions. If the culture is such that people are disciplined for making mistakes, then they might try to hide the actual problem in fear of the consequences. For example, an employee who breaks a machine might not tell his boss the truth if that boss has a reputation for terminating people who damage equipment.

Once the problem is established, potential solutions need to be generated. Some organizations encourage creative thinking for finding answers, while others have a more strict protocol. The methodology used to resolve problems stems from the culture of the organization. For example, the Catholic Church would not consider abortion as a solution to an overcrowded population problem. Abstinence is a better solution based on their culture.

Now a decision needs to be made. Some organizations have established norms regarding what can and can't be done, and those norms are embedded in the culture. For example, employees who work for an owner who is extremely frugal might know that the best decision is always the one that involves the least amount of money being spent. This is not necessarily the best choice for the company, but it stays within cultural guidelines.

The last part of the decision process involves follow up. Was the decision correct? Once again, this is driven by the culture of the organization. If the end result adheres to the philosophies and values of the culture, then it was a good choice. For example, a bakery might make a decision to throw away 500 donuts because they are more than 12 hours old. If the culture of the company is to put out high-quality products that are always fresh, then the decision was good…regardless of the money spent throwing the product in the trash. However, if the culture of that same bakery is to never waste anything, then the right decision might be to sell the donuts at a reduced cost.

Communication

Employees need to share information in order to accomplish tasks and achieve organizational goals. This can be done verbally (talking, presentation, speeches, videos, etc.) or non-verbally (body language, pictures, signs, symbols, written words, etc.), but it all falls under communication. Good communication keeps organizations healthy, while poor communicating is capable of destroying them.

Communication is an essential part of organizational culture because it influences behaviors, norms, and values. Good communication promotes a positive culture while bad communication creates the opposite effect. Leaders in progressive organizations realize this, and they regularly act to open communication lines. For example, some companies hold company, division, or department-wide meetings with upper management so employees can ask questions and gather information. Employees are able to express their opinions and beliefs to the top decision makers, and this lets them feel like they are being heard. One problem with these gatherings, however, is they can lose focus if they are too large. Due to this, some companies take an additional step and hold smaller meetings with the same goal in mind.

Open communication also leads to trust. Leaders who are aware of this survey their employees to find the level of trust in the organization. Basically, they are looking for employees' perceptions as to what the organization is like as a communication system. Poor communication leads to a lack of trust that can be difficult to restore once it is lost.

One might think that the military has a negative culture because communication is restricted and withheld in many instances. The Army, for example, often keeps information from soldiers. This type of behavior seems like it would lead to a lack of trust, but that is typically not the case. Security is an issue in the Army, and divulging certain facts could result in a crisis. Based on this, soldiers understand and accept that they are simply are better off not knowing some things…and this does not create a negative culture. In fact, the military often has a more positive culture than many of the biggest and best organizations in the world.

The role communication plays in culture is important. However, that role needs to be further broken down for a better understanding of the relationship. The following are critical areas where good communication with employees is needed in order to promote positive culture:

Employee's need for direction

Employees need guidance in order to complete the tasks expected of them and understand their roles in the organization. Without this direction, employees feel abandoned or begin to wander. This creates a culture of indecision and uncertainty.

Organizational example #1

A president of a home builder puts together a team to cut costs within the organization. If this team is assembled without being told why they have been chosen, they might not accomplish the team objectives. An engineer might not realize that he is on the team to make sure the reductions do not compromise safety. Likewise, a salesperson might not realize that she is on the team to make sure the customer will still get a quality house after the cost-cutting. The president needs to assign responsibilities to each member to prevent a culture of confusion.

Organizational example #2

Janelle is the owner of a window manufacturing company. She hires Rick to work at the factory because he has management skills that she knows can be utilized. She is not sure exactly what she wants Rick to do, so she tells him to begin work by observing the people and processes. After Rick observes for a while, Janelle wants him to tell her where he thinks his management skills are most needed.

When Rick shows up for work, other employees are confused about his job responsibilities. They don't know what he is doing, and this creates fear, confusion, and resentment for not being told why he has been hired. This also puts Rick in an uncomfortable position because he is unsure of his responsibilities. Janelle should have given Rick specific job responsibilities and made the current employees aware of those responsibilities in order to prevent cultural uncertainty.

Employee's need for honesty

Leaders need to be honest with employees in order to establish good working relationships. Employees want to hear good news and bad news because they have a vested interest in the organization. Management dishonesty leads to a lack of trust, and this results in a negative culture.

Organizational example

A computer company is buying a competitor, and the employees at the company being bought are fearful of losing their jobs during the merger. The new management is aware of these concerns, so they hold a meeting. The new leadership assures the employees that they will all have jobs for at least one year, but some changes might need to be made after that period of time. This is not necessarily good news, but the new management team's honesty allows them to build trust with the workers. This helps establish a positive culture as the merger moves forward.

Employee's need for a voice

Employees want their thoughts and concerns heard by management. Their ideas might be beneficial for the organization, and their involvement will contribute to a positive culture. This being said, discussions are a good idea before implementing workplace changes that impact employees.

Organizational example

A telephone company decides that all service personnel must wear a tie during visits to customers. They did not ask for employee input, they simply made the change because the CEO thought a dress code would create a professional appearance.

This attire change might look good, but it is not realistic. Service personnel need to run phone wires, climb poles and ladders, and go into attics...and a tie is very impractical for this type of work. In fact, a tie even presents a safety hazard if it is not carefully monitored.

This change completely demoralizes the service personnel. Some quit, some grumble silently, and others protest to management. However, the change has been made, and it is going to remain in effect. This creates a negative organizational culture that will be difficult to change.

Employee's need for praise

People like to be told they are doing a good job. This motivates them, makes them feel good about their work, and produces a positive organizational culture that influences the entire workplace. In short, a "pat on the back" goes a long way.

Organizational example

Joe works as a salesman for a barber and hair salon supply company. He normally does a good job, but last week he made a major mistake. His customer ordered 11 new custom razor blades, but Joe mistakenly entered 111 blades in the computer.

When the blades reach the warehouse, the owner Valerie calls Joe since this does not seem accurate. Joe checks his records and realizes that he made the mistake. However, the blades cannot be returned because they are custom made for a specific barber. Valerie is now stuck with $1900 worth of custom blades that none of her customers need.

Joe is upset over his mistake. However, instead of reprimanding him, Valerie tells him that this one mistake does not offset the good job he has done for the company. She thanks him for the good job he is doing, and reassures him that, in time, all of the blades will be sold to the barber who uses them.

Valerie's praise makes Joe happy about his work. Her words motivate him to try harder, and they create a positive organizational culture. If she had chosen to reprimand Joe, the effect would have been the opposite.

Employee's need for emotional intelligence

Employees have needs for empathy and compassion at work, and astute leadership has the proper skills to meet those needs. The most important aspect of those skills is emotional intelligence. Emotionally intelligent leaders have the ability to understand and communicate with their employees, and this leads to a positive organizational culture.

Organizational example

Darlene is a driver for a hazardous waste transportation company. She just found out that her father has terminal cancer, and she is visibly distraught when she shows up for work in the morning. Edwardo, the owner of the company, immediately senses her pain. He expresses his condolences and talks to her about the situation, and then he tells her to take the rest of the week off to be with her father.

Darlene appreciates Edwardo's sensitivity and understanding. He could have expressed his sorrow for the illness, and then told her to go back to work. Instead, he used emotional intelligence to comfort her in this time of need. Edwardo's actions made Darlene feel appreciated and respected, and this created a positive organizational culture for her and the employees who witnessed his compassion.

Commitment

Employees' commitment to the goals and objectives of the organization is linked to their perception of the culture. Those who perceive the culture as negative are less committed than those who perceive it as positive. Committed employees identify with the organization, and this leads to better workplace culture.

Many factors are involved in the relationship between organizational culture and organizational commitment. Let's examine some of the most important factors and their involvement:

Role conflicts

Role conflicts result when people have conflicting job responsibilities. Employees who are unsure of their responsibilities perceive the culture as stressful and often start looking for employment elsewhere. In short, role conflicts affect the commitment of employees to the organization.

Organizational example

Mary is an accounts receivable person at website designer. Martin, the owner of the company, has told her on several occasions that when there is a dispute in payment, the customer is always right. However, whenever a customer wants to take a deduction from an invoice, Martin tells Mary to argue with them about it. He becomes upset with Mary if she gives the discount... even if the customer is clearly right.

This situation is stressful for Mary. Martin tells her to behave in a certain manner, but he gets upset with her when she follows his instructions. The conflicting job responsibilities affect Mary's commitment to the organization and create a negative culture.

Empowerment

Employees who have the proper knowledge and resources to perform their work with limited supervision are empowered. They take ownership of their jobs and the processes within them, and this results in a positive perception of the culture and a strong commitment to organizational goals.

Organizational example

Marshall is a welder at an automotive assembly plant. His boss Yolanda knows that he is capable of performing his job without assistance. Yolanda simply makes sure that Marshall has the proper tools and supplies for his work, and then she leaves him alone to perform his job.

These conditions motivate Marshall to perform to the best of his ability. He works with little supervision and takes charge of all of his job-related responsibilities. Marshall is empowered, and that empowerment increases his commitment to his employer and creates a positive perception of the workplace culture.

Autonomy

Autonomy is the freedom employees have in their jobs. This is similar to empowerment, but it involves the liberty to make choices about the job rather than having the proper knowledge and resources to do the job. This results in a positive culture because people develop commitment towards their organizations.

Organizational example

Claudine is a graphic artist at an advertising company. She likes to spend Wednesday's shopping and eating lunch with her mother, so she would prefer not to work on that day. Her boss lets her take Wednesdays off and work from home on Saturday to make up the time.

This arrangement gives Claudine freedom to choose where and when she does her job. The autonomy she experiences strengthens her commitment to the company and creates a positive culture for her.

Leadership authority

Leadership authority involves the power of one person or a few select individuals to make all the decisions in an organization. Usually, these people are at the top of the hierarchy, and they limit the authority of lower level employees. When organizations place absolute power in the hands of one or a few people, they decrease employee commitment and create a negative culture.

Organizational example

Reggie is one of twenty salespeople at a lumber company. His boss, Tiffany, is the vice president of sales. Tiffany is very specific that she does not want any salespeople to make decisions without her approval. They cannot discount items, offer sales promotions, or run product advertisements without her authorization. She makes it clear that salespeople will be disciplined if they make unauthorized decisions.

Reggie feels powerless when he is with customers, and he is embarrassed that he cannot make any decisions without Tiffany's approval. This type of work situation demotivates Reggie, lowers his commitment to the organization, and promotes a negative culture.

Values

In organizations, values are very important. They influence people's decisions and behavior, and they establish norms for the entire workplace. They are the foundation of organizational culture, and they establish patterns that employees follow while performing everyday tasks.

Values originate from leadership. Their importance cannot be underestimated because they have a direct impact on significant aspects of organizational behavior including performance and ethics.

For organizations to be successful, leadership needs to align employee values and organizational values. Employees need to identify with the organization if they are expected to work toward achieving its goals and objectives. In short, strongly aligned values result in positive organizational culture.

Organizational example

Olivia works in inventory control for a furniture wholesaler. In her spare time, she volunteers at a soup kitchen close to her house. She strongly believes in giving to the less fortunate in the community.

The company Oliva works for is also philanthropic. They donate tables and chairs to local homeless shelters on a regular basis. This pleases Olivia because she needs to work for an organization that has values similar to her own, and that need is met by the furniture wholesaler.

Olivia identifies with her employer. Her values are aligned with those of the furniture wholesaler, and this enables her to have a positive perception of the organizational culture.

Management style

People are different...and this also applies to leaders. Leaders have distinctive personalities, traits, ideas, beliefs, and philosophies, and all of these factors influence the way they manage people. Management style refers to the specific methods used to manage employees.

Some leaders make decisions by themselves. They seek limited guidance from others and choose to manage using personal experience, established facts, and gut reactions. This works well when they make good decisions by reacting to the needs of the organization and employees, but wrong decisions that go unchallenged can lead to disaster.

Other leaders assume a coaching role. They provide feedback so employees understand what is needed in order to complete tasks and accomplish organizational goals. This motivates top performers, but employees that are not as capable do not always fare as well. These individuals prefer a closer supervisor/subordinate relationship, and they tend to get lost in the coaching process. Think about a basketball team. The starters are interested in the coach's feedback and the goals of the team. However, there are also players on the team who never get to play in games, and they are typically less motivated to listen to the coach and accomplish team goals.

The third type of leader lets employees make choices without interference. There is no autocratic decision making or coaching, and employees are allowed to make decisions as a team. This works well in many instances because people have the freedom to make choices. However, problems can also result. Some individuals tend to take over teams and want to make every decision, while others become social loafers who choose to let everyone else do the work.

All three of these management styles are capable of motivating or demotivating workers, and because of this, they have a direct impact on the organizational culture.

Organizational example

Isabelle and Timothy are part of a team that is working on new packaging designs for dog treats. Their boss wants the team to make all of the decisions and does not want to be involved unless they need support or guidance.

Larry is also on the team, and he is a natural leader. As soon as the group assembles, Larry takes charge. He designates roles and tells members what they need to accomplish in order to produce the new designs. Some members respond well to this takeover, but Isabelle and Timothy do not. They feel left out of the decision-making process, but they are afraid to speak up because Larry is very knowledgeable and confident.

The leadership role assumed by Larry demotivates Isabelle and Timothy. Their interest in the project becomes minimal because they do not feel like their knowledge and skills are being properly utilized. This influences their view of the organizational culture in a negative manner.

Changing culture

As noted in the introduction, culture can be difficult to change without a good plan. This is because cultural change is gradual. Barring major events or disasters, people do not change their perceptions overnight.

In order to change culture, leadership needs to be directly involved. They have to develop a vision for the change, and then implement it by being involved. Their actions will impact others in the organization, and the change will gradually come about.

One major mistake leaders make is to take themselves out of the process. They simply draw up a list of changes and turn it over to managers and human resource personnel for implementation. This does not work because employees need to see people at the top being an active part of the change.

Now that we know leadership needs to be involved and the process will take time, let's discuss what needs to be done to change organizational culture:

Start at the top

Let's revisit the importance of top management involvement. Some leaders implement "do as I say, not as I do" cultural change policies. These do not work and will never be effective because culture involves perception. Employees can be forced to behave in certain ways and conform to new standards, but they cannot be coerced into changing their perceptions. Workplace experiences influence cultural perception, and that perception will be negative if employees see leaders ignoring their own rules. In short, top management needs to change their own behavior if they want others to do the same.

Organizational example

Leadership at a company wants to change the culture to one that cares about the local community. They begin to give money to poor families, and they offer to match any employee donations that are posted on a designated bulletin board. Executives at the company start the process by pledging $200 each on the board. This is a show of good faith and the chance of getting lower-level employees to donate increases based on the perception that management is practicing what they preach.

Explain the change

Employees want to know why the culture needs to change. This is completely understandable because work is an important aspect of their lives. Management needs to explain the reasons for the change and get employees involved. Involvement is critical because a change in culture is dependent on a change in behavior, and it is difficult for employees to change their behavior if they are a distant part of the process.

Organizational example

Leadership at a company wants to change the culture to one that is focused on sound ethical principles. They schedule a meeting with all of the employees to explain that certain purchasing agents were taking illegal gifts for preferential treatment of vendors. These individuals have been terminated, but the company wants everyone to be more focused on ethical behavior. To accomplish this, an outside consultant has been hired, and all employees will go through ethical training. Employees are encouraged to ask questions, and management answers them with honesty in order to explain exactly why the change is taking place. In short, the change is explained in a meeting, and the employees will be involved in training.

Communicate throughout

Let employees know how things are going during the entire progress. They need to know what has transpired and what will occur next. This helps maintain focus on the task at hand, and it keeps employees interested. It is achieved by providing information, facts, data, and accomplishments.

Organizational example

Leadership at a company wants to change the culture to one that is more customer oriented. Every month, they send out an email to everyone in the organization to let them know how things are progressing. The following information is always included in the email:

- The number of customer complaints and the percent increase or decrease from the prior month
- The correct order fulfillment rates and the percent increase or decrease from the prior month
- The results from customer surveys and the rating increase or decrease from the prior month

Employees are also encouraged to ask management questions about new developments so they are not left wondering what has transpired. In short, progress of the change implantation is updated throughout the process.

Reward achievements

As employees embrace the change, management needs to highlight their accomplishments using rewards. These rewards do not have to be monetary, but employees who behave in the desired manner need a spotlight put on their actions. Sometimes a simple acknowledgment does the job.

Organizational example

Leadership at a company wants to change the culture to one where everyone arrives for work and meetings in a timelier manner. They schedule an 8:00 am meeting on Monday morning and everyone arrives on time. The manager in charge of the meeting acknowledges this fact and thanks everyone by providing donuts and coffee. This small token of appreciation rewards the achievement of being punctual. In short, this group of employees behaved in a desired manner, and their behavior was acknowledged and rewarded.

After the culture has been successfully changed, it needs to be monitored. Internal audits should be conducted periodically to assure that behavior is not reverting back to old ways. Surveys can be issued to get a snapshot of what is transpiring, but it is often easier and less expensive to ask employees questions during everyday conversation. Under relaxed conditions, people are typically very honest about their workplace perceptions.

Summary

All organizations have unique experiences, philosophies, behaviors, norms, and values that define them and make up their culture. That culture provides guidelines for every employee, and it starts at the top of the organizational hierarchy.

This book examines the concept of organizational culture, the relationship it has with other variables, and the best ways to change it. It provides understanding using insightful analysis, and workplace examples are utilized throughout for real-world application. In short, the information provided increases the reader's knowledge about this very significant aspect of organizational behavior.

www.ingramcontent.com/pod-product-compliance
Lightning Source LLC
Chambersburg PA
CBHW070337190526
45169CB00005B/1939